Francis Frith's
London

Photographic Memories

Francis Frith's
London

Terence Sackett

First published in the United Kingdom in 1998
by WBC Ltd

Revised paperback edition published in the United Kingdom in 2000
by Frith Book Company Ltd
ISBN 1-85937-183-3

Reprinted in Paperback 2002
ISBN 1-85937-183-3

British Library Cataloguing in Publication Data

Francis Frith's London
Terence Sackett

Frith Book Company Ltd
Frith's Barn, Teffont,
Salisbury, Wiltshire SP3 5QP
Tel: +44 (0) 1722 716 376
Email: info@francisfrith.co.uk
www.francisfrith.co.uk

Printed and bound in Great Britain

Contents

Francis Frith: *Victorian Pioneer*

FRANCIS FRITH, Victorian founder of the world-famous photographic archive, was a complex and multitudinous man. A devout Quaker and a highly successful Victorian businessman, he was both philosophic by nature and pioneering in outlook.

By 1855 Francis Frith had already established a wholesale grocery business in Liverpool, and sold it for the astonishing sum of £200,000, which is the equivalent today of over £15,000,000. Now a multi-millionaire, he was able to indulge his passion for travel. As a child he had pored over travel books written by early explorers, and his fancy and imagination had been stirred by family holidays to the sublime mountain regions of Wales and Scotland. 'What a land of spirit-stirring and enriching scenes and places!' he had written. He was to return to these scenes of grandeur in later years to 'recapture the thousands of vivid and tender memories', but with a different purpose. Now in his thirties, and captivated by the new science of photography, Frith set out on a series of pioneering journeys to the Nile regions that occupied him from 1856 until 1860.

Intrigue and Adventure

He took with him on his travels a specially-designed wicker carriage that acted as both dark-room and sleeping chamber. These far-flung journeys were packed with intrigue and adventure. In his life story, written when he was sixty-three, Frith tells of being held captive by bandits, and of fighting 'an awful midnight battle to the very point of surrender with a deadly pack of hungry, wild dogs'. Sporting flowing Arab costume, Frith arrived at Akaba by camel seventy years before Lawrence, where he encountered 'desert princes and rival sheikhs, blazing with jewel-hilted swords'.

During these extraordinary adventures he was assiduously exploring the desert regions bordering the Nile and patiently recording the antiquities and peoples with his camera. He was the first photographer to venture beyond the sixth cataract. Africa was still the mysterious 'Dark Continent', and Stanley and Livingstone's historic meeting was a decade into the future. The conditions for picture taking confound belief. He laboured for hours in his wicker dark-room in the sweltering heat of the desert, while the volatile chemicals fizzed dangerously in their trays. Often he was forced to work in remote tombs and caves where conditions were cooler. Back in London he exhibited his photographs and was 'rapturously cheered' by members of the Royal Society. His reputation as a photographer was made overnight. An eminent modern historian has likened their impact on the population of the time to that on our own generation of the first photographs taken on the surface of the moon.

Venture of a Life-Time

Characteristically, Frith quickly spotted the opportunity to create a new business as a specialist publisher of photographs. He lived in an era of immense and sometimes violent change. For the poor in the early part of Victoria's reign work was a drudge and the hours long, and people had precious little free time to enjoy themselves. Most had no transport other than a cart or gig at their disposal, and had not travelled far beyond the boundaries of their own town or village. However, by the 1870s, the railways had threaded their way across the country, and Bank Holidays and half-day Saturdays had been made obligatory by Act of Parliament. All of a sudden the ordinary working man and his family were able to enjoy days out and see a little more of the world.

With characteristic business acumen, Francis Frith foresaw that these new tourists would enjoy having souvenirs to commemorate their days out. In 1860 he married Mary Ann Rosling and set out with the intention of photographing every city, town and village in Britain. For the next thirty years he travelled the country by train and by pony and trap, producing fine photographs of seaside resorts and beauty spots that were keenly bought by millions of Victorians. These prints were painstakingly pasted into family albums and pored over during the dark nights of winter, rekindling precious memories of summer excursions.

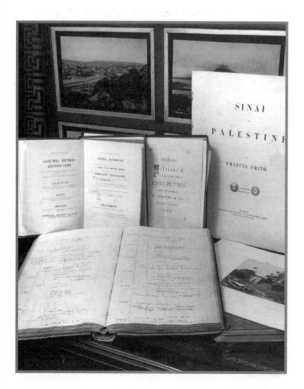

The Rise of Frith & Co

Frith's studio was soon supplying retail shops all over the country. To meet the demand he gathered about him a small team of photographers, and published the work of independent artist-photographers of the calibre of Roger Fenton and Francis Bedford. In order to gain some understanding of the scale of Frith's business one only has to look at the catalogue issued by Frith & Co in 1886: it runs to some 670 pages, listing not only many thousands of views of the British Isles but also many photographs of most European countries, and China, Japan, the USA and

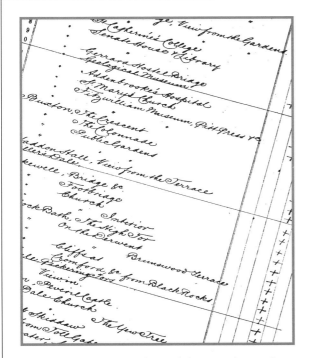

Canada – note the sample page shown above from the hand-written *Frith & Co* ledgers detailing pictures taken. By 1890 Frith had created the greatest specialist photographic publishing company in the world, with over 2,000 outlets – more than the combined number that Boots and WH Smith have today! The picture on the right shows the *Frith & Co* display board at Ingleton in the Yorkshire Dales. Beautifully constructed with mahogany frame and gilt inserts, it could display up to a dozen local scenes.

Postcard Bonanza

The ever-popular holiday postcard we know today took many years to develop. In 1870 the Post Office issued the first plain cards, with a pre-printed stamp on one face. In 1894 they allowed other publishers' cards to be sent through the mail with an attached adhesive halfpenny stamp. Demand grew rapidly, and in 1895 a new size of postcard was permitted called the court card, but there was little room for illustration. In 1899, a year after Frith's death, a new card measuring 5.5 x 3.5 inches became the standard format, but it was not until 1902 that the divided back came into being, with address and message on one face and a full-size illustration on the other. *Frith & Co* were in the vanguard of postcard development, and Frith's sons Eustace and Cyril continued their father's monumental task, expanding the number of views offered to the public and recording more and more places in Britain, as the coasts and countryside were opened up to mass travel.

Francis Frith died in 1898 at his villa in Cannes, his great project still growing. The archive he created continued in business for another seventy years. By 1970 it contained over a third of a million pictures of 7,000 cities, towns and villages. The massive photographic record Frith has left to us stands as a living monument to a special and very remarkable man.

Frith's Archive: *A Unique Legacy*

FRANCIS FRITH'S legacy to us today is of immense significance and value, for the magnificent archive of evocative photographs he created provides a unique record of change in 7,000 cities, towns and villages throughout Britain over a century and more. Frith and his fellow studio photographers revisited locations many times down the years to update their views, compiling for us an enthralling and colourful pageant of British life and character.

We tend to think of Frith's sepia views of Britain as nostalgic, for most of us use them to conjure up memories of places in our own lives with which we have family associations. It often makes us forget that to Francis Frith they were records of daily life as it was actually being lived in the cities, towns and villages of his day. The Victorian age was one of great and often bewildering change for ordinary people, and though the pictures evoke an impression of slower times, life was as busy and hectic as it is today.

We are fortunate that Frith was a photographer of the people, dedicated to recording the minutiae of everyday life. For it is this sheer wealth of visual data, the painstaking chronicle of changes in dress, transport, street layouts, buildings, housing, engineering and landscape that captivates us so much today. His remarkable images offer us a powerful link with the past and with the lives of our ancestors.

Today's Technology

Computers have now made it possible for Frith's many thousands of images to be accessed almost instantly. In the Frith archive today, each photograph is carefully 'digitised' then stored on a CD Rom. Frith archivists can locate a single photograph amongst thousands within seconds. Views can be catalogued and sorted under a variety of categories of place and content to the immediate benefit of researchers.

Inexpensive reference prints can be created for them at the touch of a mouse button, and a wide range of books and other printed materials assembled and published for a wider, more general readership - in the next twelve months over a hundred Frith local history titles will be published! The day-to-day workings of the archive are very different from how they were in Francis Frith's time: imagine the herculean task of sorting through eleven tons of glass negatives as Frith had to do to locate a particular

THE FRANCIS FRITH COLLECTION
Photographic publishers since 1860

HOME | PHOTO SEARCH | BOOKS | PORTFOLIO | GALLERY | MY CART
Products | History | Other Collections | Contact us | Help?

your town,
your village

365,000
photographs of 7,000 towns and villages, taken between 1860 & 1970.

The Frith Archive
The Frith Archive is the remarkable legacy of its energetic and visionary founder. Today, the Frith archive is the only nationally important archive of its kind still in private ownership.

The Collection is world-renowned for the extraordinary quality of its images.

The Gallery
This month The Frith Gallery features images from "Frith's Egypt".

News...
Image update complete.
An additional 5,000 images have been added and the quality of all images has now been improved.

Sample Chapters available.
The first selection of sample chapters from the Frith Book Co.'s extensive range is now available. All are offered in Pdf format for easy downloading and viewing.

explore
FRITH
Search thousands of photographs from one of the worlds' great archives.

Town search

GO

County search
Select a county

GO

the FRITHgallery

See Frith at www.francisfrith.co.uk

sequence of pictures! Yet the archive still prides itself on maintaining the same high standards of excellence laid down by Francis Frith, including the painstaking cataloguing and indexing of every view.

It is curious to reflect on how the internet now allows researchers in America and elsewhere greater instant access to the archive than Frith himself ever enjoyed. Many thousands of individual views can be called up on screen within seconds on one of the Frith internet sites, enabling people living continents away to revisit the streets of their ancestral home town, or view places in Britain where they have enjoyed holidays. Many overseas researchers welcome the chance to view special theme selections, such as transport, sports, costume and ancient monuments.

We are certain that Francis Frith would have heartily approved of these modern developments in imaging techniques, for he himself was always working at the very limits of Victorian photographic technology.

The Value of the Archive Today

Because of the benefits brought by the computer, Frith's images are increasingly studied by social historians, by researchers into genealogy and ancestory, by architects, town planners, and by teachers and schoolchildren involved in local history projects.

In addition, the archive offers every one of us an opportunity to examine the places where we and our families have lived and worked down the years. Highly successful in Frith's own era, the archive is now, a century and more on, entering a new phase of popularity.

The Past in Tune with the Future

Historians consider the Francis Frith Collection to be of prime national importance. It is the only archive of its kind remaining in private ownership and has been valued at a million pounds. However, this figure is now rapidly increasing as digital technology enables more and more people around the world to enjoy its benefits.

Francis Frith's archive is now housed in an historic timber barn in the beautiful village of Teffont in Wiltshire. Its founder would not recognize the archive office as it is today. In place of the many thousands of dusty boxes containing glass plate negatives and an all-pervading odour of photographic chemicals, there are now ranks of computer screens. He would be amazed to watch his images travelling round the world at unimaginable speeds through network and internet lines.

The archive's future is both bright and exciting. Francis Frith, with his unshakeable belief in making photographs available to the greatest number of people, would undoubtedly approve of what is being done today with his lifetime's work. His photographs, depicting our shared past, are now bringing pleasure and enlightenment to millions around the world a century and more after his death.

London - An Introduction

Until the end of the 18th century London was a compact city. Its merchants lived in the square mile and the aristocracy in the more fashionable areas of Piccadilly and the West End.

Beyond Park Lane, however, there was a wilderness of forest and mire, where footpads and highwayman lurked. Londoners were regularly accosted in the Strand. Many preferred to travel by water on the River Thames.

In the Victorian era the city grew at an extraordinary rate as the Empire spread and wealth returned to the coffers of the London banks. Whole neighbourhoods of ramshackle housing were demolished and the great thoroughfares we know today were created. Nash remodelled much of the West End, and great houses and mansions lined the leafy thoroughfares that were once grazing land for the city's flocks of sheep. Public spaces such as Trafalgar Square and Piccadilly Circus were created and richly embellished by public sculpture and memorials commemorating Britain's historic past.

The 1851 Great Exhibition symbolised the country's new wealth and prestige. The great glass halls conceived by Paxton were filled to bursting with triumphs of industry and engineering endeavour, and the world flocked to enjoy a glimpse of the exciting future.

The City of London developed gradually into the centre of world finance. London's burgeoning banks and insurance companies clamoured for space in the overcrowded square mile. Further widespread demolition followed, and new streets of Victorian Gothic offices were constructed, heavy and sepulchral in character. Here many thousands of clerks and office workers laboured day in and day out. Traffic congested the newly built or refurbished roads and bridges and Londoners struggled with the complexities of city life very much as we do today.

The poor were ever present. Thousands of country people flocked to London with the promise of work. Yet with increasing mechanisation of production traditional crafts and trades were swiftly superseded, throwing thousands into the streets to earn a few shillings. London's street traders were a legend, their guile and cunning offering them the only hope of survival in a hostile city.

For centuries London's wealth had been fuelled by river traffic. Great ships plied the estuary of the Thames to unload at the many new docks that were constructed as far upriver as

London Bridge. The wharves and quays resounded with the cries of stevedores and dock workers unloading coal, timber and the raw materials of engineering. There were also exotic imports from China and Asia to tempt the wealthy.

By the time of Queen Victoria's Jubilee in 1897 the face of the capital would have been almost unrecognisable to an eighteenth century Londoner. The streets and buildings stretched out into the countryside and millions of people had moved out of the expensive centre to newly-built suburbs to become commuters. The rate of change had been bewildering and relentless. Everyone was touched by it and many suffered as a result of it. Yet there was no going back. London's expansion has never slowed since. With its beautiful streets and buildings, and its unique position as financial centre of Europe and the colonies, it had justly earned its reputation as the greatest city in the world.

Along the River

Today the Thames is a little more than an obstacle for Londoners to cross. Commuters funnel over its old bridges towards the railway stations and suburbs. The river slides by below the parapets keeping its own counsel.

In Victorian times the river was the vital lifeline of the city, thronged with ships. Vessels sailed and steamed down the estuary to offload their cargoes at bustling docks all the way down to London Bridge. The quays were noisy with the cries of stevedores and labourers shifting coals and every manner of import and export. Smaller craft plied upriver, carrying produce to Thames-side towns and into the canals that threaded their way through the Midlands to the north.

With the coming of the railways and the motor vehicle the Thames entered a period of gradual and painful decline. Now it is almost the exclusive province of tourists who enjoy the vistas of the City from its breezy waters.

Cheyne Walk 1890 L130087
A carriage with top-hatted coachman waits patiently outside one of Cheyne Walk's many grand Georgian brick houses. Graceful plane trees screen residents from the more boisterous life on the water. A fleet of barges, their sales furled, are berthed at the quay.

Cheyne Walk, Chelsea 1890 L130084
This tranquil street of handsome houses fringing the river was built in 1708. Chelsea had long been the haunt of artists and writers - Thomas Carlyle lived at 5, Cheyne Walk for almost half a century. Other illustrious residents, including Philip Wilson Steer, Whistler and Rossetti, were his close neighbours. Boats squat in the mud under the embankment.

Albert Bridge c1900 L130129
Until 1878 all but three of the bridges over the Thames were owned by private companies who levelled tolls on foot passengers. In 1879 this beautiful bridge of three airy spans, topped with decorative towers, was made free for public access.

Chelsea Embankment 1890 L130083
The Thames Embankment, which skirts the front of Cheyne Walk, was created by Sir Joseph Bazalgette. Constructed over mud flats, it conceals the sewers that were once a scourge of the locality. The barge in the photograph, its sail furled, is loaded with straw. These old vessels were vital carriers of coal, fruit, vegetables and building materials from Kent, Essex and other east-coast ports.

◄ **Westminster Bridge c1900** L130303
This fine bridge is one of the most dazzling structures spanning London's river and was constructed in 1862 at the cost of £250,000. With the waters at low tide as they are here, critics have suggested the bridge has an ungraceful 'lanky' appearance. Its uniquely light construction was the cause of trepidation amongst Londoners, for passengers on horse drawn buses felt an unnerving vibration under the wheels as they passed over.

◄ Lambeth Riverside 1880

L130120

This Lambeth river frontage presents a very different face to the more refined Chelsea scene across the river. Here is a clutter of ramshackle warehouses, timber-yards and wharves. The flimsy houses were clearly not designed to face the water, for the windows are few and diminutive. The crumbling facades bring a clear impression of neglect and poverty.

▼ Victoria Embankment 1890

L130189

A steamer, with a party of sightseers on board, has just left the quay heading down river. The women cluster at the stern under parasols. A little further along on the left is Cleopatra's Needle. This far-famed monument was transported to Britain through the treacherous Bay of Biscay from the deserts of Egypt, where it had lain buried and forgotten in the sands. It took considerable ingenuity to erect it in such a close space, for it is almost seventy feet in height.

◄ Old Waterloo Bridge 1895 L130052

Gulls forage for food in the frozen wastes. The ice has broken and the waters of the river released. Canova considered the old Waterloo Bridge, with its nine elliptical arches, to be one of the most magnificent in Europe. Originally called Strand Bridge, it was opened in 1817 on the anniversary of the Battle of Waterloo.

▼ Old Waterloo Bridge 1902 L130155

This panorama of the river through broad lawns and lofty trees reveals the bridge's graceful character. Engineered by John Rennie, it was well over 1,000 feet long and surmounted by an open balustrade. In 1924, after engineering reports of a dangerous weakening of one of the main arches, the old bridge was closed to traffic. Work on the new Waterloo Bridge was started in 1937.

▼ Waterfront by St Paul's 1890 L130017

This famous vista, taken from Bankside, shows the glorious dome of St Paul's rising over the roofs of London. The river is edged not with the anonymous and monumental office blocks we see today but with a pleasing clutter of wharves and warehouses. The river was a populous place of work where barges and a thousand other vessels plied. On the right is the colliery wharf of the Weardale Iron and Coal Company.

▲ Embankment from Temple Pier 1890

L130077

The delightful Temple Gardens once extended right the way down to the river. Here were clipped green lawns and exquisite quadrangles. The fortunate few could enjoy a few precious moments away from the bustle of the city streets above. The imposing arch is in the monumental Egyptian style. In the background is Waterloo Bridge.

◀ Blackfriars Bridge 1890

L130070

The halfpenny toll on the original Blackfriars Bridge caused riots, and in 1780 angry protesters burned down the toll-house. After a succession of expensive repairs a replacement was suggested, and the present bridge was erected in 1864 at a cost of £265,000. With its colossal piers, and recesses set on pillars of polished Aberdeen granite, Blackfriars Bridge has been censured by critics for being 'gaudy'.

London Bridge c1900
L130317
This five-arched granite structure was constructed in 1827 from the designs of John Rennie. Its excessive cost was once the talk of the city. Estimates ran as high as two and a half million pounds. In 1869 it was faced with cubes of Aberdeen granite. In the background is the imposing column of the Monument.

London Bridge 1890 L130034
The traffic jam is clearly not a modern phenomenon. London Bridge is thronged with cabs, carriers, brewers' drays, hay wagons, omnibuses and carriages. An dense procession of top-hatted gentlemen hurry along the pavement to their city offices. London Bridge's lamp-posts were cast from the metal of French cannons captured in the Peninsula War.

London Bridge c1890 L130178
So busy was London bridge at peak times that the authorities were compelled to station police constables along the central rib of the roadway to encourage a smooth flow of traffic. All vehicles moving at walking pace were ushered abruptly to the kerb sides so that swifter carriages could enjoy a clear passage.

Opening of Tower Bridge 1894 L130019
The bridge was formally opened with great pomp and ceremony on 30 June 1894. The flags are flying on the steamers, one of which is being hauled along by a tugboat. These pleasure craft are packed to the gunwhales with dignitaries celebrating the great event.

◀ **Tower Bridge 1894**

L130046

A steam tugboat hauls a barge into the docks on the right. St Katharine's Dock was built in 1828. Some of the dock developments were massive in scale, revealing the scale of shipping using the Thames. The West India Docks on the Isle of Dogs could receive up to six hundred ships.

▼ Tower Bridge c1895 L130519
The raised footway at the top of the towers, 140 feet above the level of the river, was closed in 1909 after a spate of suicides. In the foreground lies the Pool of London, the province of London watermen for generations. The river, at the end of Victoria's reign, is still busy with flat barges and sailing ships. In the background are the pinnacles of the Tower of London.

▼ Tower Bridge 1910 L130058
Where London's other bridges are dignified and utilitarian, Tower Bridge, with its 'daring majesty' cocks a snook at Victorian formality. Barry permitted Sir Horace Jones to encase his steel skeleton in stone until it resembled an iced cake. Mock Gothic turrets were added, a profusion of sharply arched windows and much other sham detailing. To many the stupendous structure had the look of an ornate medieval castle.

◄ Tower Bridge Opening c1895 L130061
Uniquely for London bridges, the bascules of Tower Bridge can be raised or lowered to permit the passage of high-peaked vessels. Driven by steam, the hydraulic machinery hoisted the heavy 1,000 ton bascules to their raised positions in two minutes.

▼ Thames Shipbuilding c1910 L130056

It is dawn and stevedores, carpenters, coopers and ropemakers are arriving by boat to begin the day's toil. They clamber eagerly up the rickety steps to stake their claim to work - most were poorly-paid casual workers hired daily. The thicket of wooden scaffolds would give a modern-day health and safety inspector a heart attack.

▼ Old Ferry Wharf c1890 L130085

The cityside banks of the Thames were busy with stevedores and dockers during the Victorian era, for London's river had been the source of its prosperity for centuries. However, by 1910 the industry was parlously overmanned, and the docks had gone into sharp decline.

▲ Thames Wharf 1910
L130057

Henry Mayhew describes a typical dockside scene: 'The cooper is hammering at the casts on the quay; the chains of the cranes, loosed of their weight, rattle as they fly up; the ropes splash in the water; some captain shouts his orders...'
The noise of all the cranes and machinery must have been deafening, far louder than London's traffic today.

◀ **A Thames Wharfside View c1886** L130185
In this ramshackle scene, flat-bottomed coal barges squat in the mud alongside a collier's wharf. By 1850 much of the coal hauled to London from the Northern coalfields was offloaded by steam power. Yet upriver, above London Bridge, were the more modest colliers, whose simple barges, loaded by man-power, carried consignments on to Thameside towns, for shipment to the Midlands and the north through the canal network.

The West End

The West End has long been the most fashionable region of London. Simply having an address there was an advantage. Robert Southey said that his tailor lived at the West End of Town, 'and consequently he is supposed to make my coat in a better style of fashion'.

The West End streets were designed and created by Britain's most celebrated architects, men of calibre and vision, such as Wren, Nash and Inigo Jones. The magnificent thoroughfares like the Strand, Piccadilly and Regent Street are world-renowned, and the great and the good promenaded their pavements savouring the delights of fashionable hotels, restaurants and art galleries. The mansions of Mayfair and the clubs of Pall Mall were the place to impress and be impressed. Broad, leafy squares offered the wealthy peace and tranquillity in the very midst of the 'monstrous city'. Great public spaces like Trafalgar Square, Piccadilly and the parks drew crowds of Londoners for civic events and occasions. They cheered and roared their approval as royalty processed in stately fashion from their palaces into the public streets.

Cheyne Walk 1890 L130086
Away from the boisterous life of the river, Cheyne Walk, with its narrow, balconied houses and modish shops, was a haven of gentility, dedicated to refined if somewhat Bohemian pursuits. In the background is Chelsea Old Church, which suffered extensive bomb damage in the War.

Waterman's Arms, Chelsea 1875 L130123
In narrow alleys leading down to the river, similar to the one depicted here, there was an abundance of small taverns and public houses catering for the working man. Bargemen from the fleets that tied up below came here after the day's toil for conversation and community.

Rotten Row 1890 L130171
Hyde Park has been called London's park 'par excellence'. Rotten Row, a corruption of route du roi, was a ride set aside for equestrians and fashionable promenaders. During afternoons in the London season, it was densely thronged with carriages parading their smart passengers around at little more than walking pace. The inevitable more refined traffic jams ended in polite deadlock.

Park Lane 1890 L130166
Park Lane, once the desolate by-road known as Tiburn Lane, was a refined street of palatial mansions enjoying expansive vistas of the Park. These great houses included Grosvenor House, the home of the Marquess of Westminster, Holdernesse House, the residence of the Marquess of Londonderry, and Dorchester House.

Hyde Park 1890
L130105
Hyde Park extends from
Piccadilly westwards to
Kensington Gardens. Its
360-acres of open
green space were called
by William Pitt 'the lung
of London'. 'Here',
writes Thomas Miller,
'the pride and beauty of
England may be seen
upon their own stage;
and on a fine day in the
season no other spot in
the world can outrival in
rich display and chaste
grandeur the scene
which is here
presented'.

◄ **The Wellington Arch, Hyde Park Corner 1915**
L130202
The arch of this impressive monument was originally crowned by Wyatt's colossal equestrian statue of the England's military darling, the Iron Duke. In the 1880s, when the French wars were long forgotten, it was moved to Aldershot and replaced by the dramatic bronze by Adrian Jones, an allegorical rendering of Peace dropping out of the heavens onto the chariot of war.

◄ Park Lane 1900 L130035
This graceful ornamental fountain was erected in 1875 at the southern end of Park Lane at the junction with Hamilton Place. Designed by Sir Hamo Thornycroft, it incorporates three heroic-size marble figures of Shakespeare, Milton and Chaucer. The statue is surmounted by the gilded bronze winged figure of Fame, poised with one foot on a globe.

▼ Hyde Park Corner c1900
L130169
Only a century and a half ago Hyde Park was bordered by mire and wilderness. Londoners tended market gardens close by which are now smothered by the buildings of Kensington. In the 18th century it was considered foolhardy to venture here after dark. Travellers joined forces to ward off the attentions of highwaymen.

◄ Hyde Park Corner c1910 L130003
Decimus Burton's impressive arch is topped by a decorative frieze depicting horsemen, the design imitated from the Elgin Marbles which were on display in the British Museum. So much of this luxurious neighbourhood mimics the glories of classical Greece.

Hyde Park Corner c1908 L130151
The handsome triple-arched gateway, with its classical screen and groups of Ionic columns, was intended originally to create a noble approach to the Park from Buckingham Palace. It was designed and built in 1828 by Decimus Burton. The omnibus on the right, heading for Pimlico, is advertising the famous furnishing and decorating emporium of Maples.

▼ Apsley House, Piccadilly c1920 L130238

To the right of the arch is Apsley House, one of only two or three of Piccadilly's great houses to survive. Known popularly as 'Number One, London', it was built by Robert Adam in the 1770s. It was bought by the Duke of Wellington in 1817 and here were held the glittering banquets celebrating the victory at Waterloo until his death in 1852.

▼ Piccadilly 1910 L130051

This illustrious thoroughfare was once one of the two main routes leading westwards out of London. Because of its proximity to open parkland the wealthy clamoured to move here. From the 18th century onwards houses and shops were built that were to bring the street its reputation for refined living. In Piccadilly are the stylish Burlington and Piccadilly Arcades, the Ritz, and the Royal Academy.

▲ Buckingham Palace c1890 L130173

In the time of James I the leafy grounds where this celebrated royal palace now stands grew mulberry bushes for the silk industry. The palace was built in its original form in the early 1700s and adapted to the Palladian style by John Nash in the 1830s. The Lord Chamberlain was always inundated with requests to view from the public, but permits were only granted to view the royal stables.

◄ **Buckingham Palace and
The Mall c1955** L1305050
Marble Arch stood here in
the Mall until 1850, when it
was removed to its present
position at the top of Park
Lane. The Mall, an expan-
sive and formal approach to
the Palace, is fringed with
limes, planes and elms, and
skirts the north side of the
diminutive St James's Park.
Here, in freezing winters,
Londoners enjoyed skating
on the pond.

Piccadilly Circus 1890 L130002
This famous junction was once known as Regent Circus and developed out of Nash's elegant modelling of Regent Street. George IV likened Piccadilly Circus to an illusion of preventing 'the sensation of crossing Piccadilly being perceived'. In 1886 many of its buildings were demolished and the open space considerably enlarged.

Piccadilly Circus 1890 L130036
Dominating this view is the classical portico of the London Pavilion, one wing of which was occupied by the Piccadilly Restaurant. Here the well-heeled flocked to dine. It is hard to believe that this elegant corner of the West End is now smothered with giant neon advertisements. Opposite is the Criterion Restaurant, 'in whose spacious saloons one may rub shoulders with the representatives of every civilised nation'.

Eros and Piccadilly Circus 1887 L130186
The glittering fountain depicting Eros was a memorial to the philanthropic nobleman Lord Shaftesbury. He died in 1886 and this photograph shows the fountain soon after it was erected. It was designed by Sir Alfred Gilbert, and when challenged about its impropriety at the time, supporters pointed out that it was 'purely symbolical and illustrative of Christian charity'.

**Piccadilly Circus
c1890** L130038
The city's horse-drawn
omnibuses were
operated by the London
General Company. This
Brixton Church to
Charing Cross service
was identified by its
green coachwork. To
tread the stage of the
London Pavilion, shown
behind, was the loftiest
ambition of the music
hall artiste. The
Piccadilly Restaurant
has been taken over by
the Spaten Beer
Company.

◀ **Piccadilly Circus 1890**
L130002
Loafers of all kinds sit on the steps under Eros. The tradition for oversized hoardings and signboards has already been set. Mellin's Foods and Perrier Water shout their sales messages across the expansive space.

◀ Regent Street and The Quadrant 1900 L130163

Conceived and built by John Nash in 1813, this famous thoroughfare has been said to represent 'the highest beauty of street architecture. The bold, sweeping curve of the Quadrant originally incorporated an open Doric arcade of 270 columns supporting a balustraded roof. However, the heavy cast shadows attracted 'undesirable company' and the arcade was eventually removed in 1848.

▼ Regent Street c1890 L130079

This view looks north towards Oxford Street. Nash's handsome terraces were spurned by London's affluent classes, for stucco was considered common. Some said that his glorious creation was compromised by poor building work, but all agreed that Nash conjured for this region of the West End a genteel and polished atmosphere that has considerably added to its prosperity down the years.

◀ Regent Circus 1890 L130206

This central section of Regent Street follows the line of the old Swallow Street, where London's notorious highwaymen left their horses in livery. The street rigidly defined the neighbourhoods of rich and poor. To the west were the homes of society families and to the east a poor and wretched neighbourhood, part of which became Soho. In the foreground is a Hurdy Gurdy man.

▼ **The National Gallery from Duncannon Street 1897** L130054
The paintings that formed the basis of Britain's national collection were purchased for £57,000 in 1824 from J Angerstein. The exhibition halls created on the north side of Trafalgar Square to display the lavish canvases were not universally admired. One Victorian critic believed 'the authorities showed a frugal mind in the low elevation of the building with its pepper-box turrets and insignificant dome'.

▼ **Regent Street 1900** L130225
A contemporary guidebook suggests that in Regent Street were to be found 'pedestrians of every class, from the fashionable lounger to the street Arab; from the duchess to the work-girl; ... the bewigged and padded roué...; from the quietly-dressed English gentleman to the flashily-arrayed foreign count of doubtful antecedents'.

▲ **St Martin-in-the-Fields Church, Trafalgar Square 1890**
L130133
This exquisite Royal church was designed and erected by the architect James Gibbs in the 1720s. The expansive portico is generally admired, but the heavy steeple is said to lack elegance. Nell Gwynne was buried here.

◀ **Trafalgar Square 1908**
L130152
This is arguably the most famous public open space in the world. Sir Robert Peel called it 'one of the finest sites in Europe'. It was created in the 1830s on the site of the King's Mews and a jumble of decrepit buildings known popularly as Bermuda, Caribee, and Porridge Islands, where the poor of London frequented a plethora of cheap cook-shops.

Trafalgar Square 1890 L130190
Trafalgar Square, largely because of its huge size and central position, became a popular place for Londoners to gather. On Sunday 13 November 1887, a crowd of twenty thousand was dispersed by the Life Guards and Grenadier Guards with fixed bayonets, after defying a police order against public processions approaching the square on Sunday.

Trafalgar Square 1890 L130161
Nelson's column was not the first choice of monument to embellish Trafalgar Square - a Colonel Trench had proposed a great pyramid to dwarf St Paul's. Of Portland stone, and 145 feet high, it was erected in 1843. The figure of Nelson was carved from three massive stones, the largest of which weighed thirty tons.

Trafalgar Square 1900 L130062
Four immense bronze lions by Landseer guard the foot of the memorial. The fountains, conceived by Sir Charles Barry, were considered by some Victorians to detract from the overall magnificence of the monument, 'because of the ridiculous insufficiency of their jets of water'.

St Giles 1885 L130215
It is difficult to tell what these traders are selling, but it is probably wet fish. It looks as if they have almost cleared their tray. A young boy pauses on his way to buy a jug of beer. The commercial streets of the West End were always thronged with street traders pushing their handcarts, who returned at nights to slum areas of the East End.

St Giles Circus 1910

L130218

A bustling street scene at the junction of Oxford Street and the Charing Cross Road. We think of advertising as a modern phenomenon. Yet the Victorian businessman was never slow nor discreet in proclaiming his sales message. These omnibuses are smothered in posters for legendary brands - Dewar's Whisky, Schweppes, Pears Soap, and Swan Vestas.

Westminster Abbey c1867 L130142

This sublime abbey, scene of many coronations down the centuries, is probably the most famous of English religious buildings, and considered the pinnacle of European Gothic. Henry II began the reshaping of Edward the Confessor's old church. Restyling continued until well into the 16th century. The abbey was embellished by its lofty twin towers in the early 1700s.

Westminster Abbey 1908 L130150
Behind are Big Ben and the Houses of Parliament. In the foreground is the Westminster Column, an imposing monument of red granite, designed by Gilbert Scott, in memory of scholars of Westminster School who had fallen in the Crimea. Four imposing lions crouch at its base.

Houses of Parliament 1886 L130188
This 'superb temple of legislation' in Tudor Gothic was built to replace the old medieval Palace which burned down in 1834. Covering nearly eight acres of ground, it was constructed to Sir Charles Barry's design, although its intricate ornament and detailing were conceived and wrought by that master of Victorian Gothic, Augustus Pugin.

Houses of Parliament 1908 L130149
The finest prospect of Barry's Palace of Westminster is to be enjoyed from the river, where the facade extends to a length of almost a thousand feet. The strong vertical detailing was clearly intended to create the impression of a just and God-fearing Parliament aspiring to the Heavenly virtues.

Houses of Parliament 1890 L130162
In 1848 a serious drainage problem was discovered inside the Parliament building. A main sewer, passing directly underneath, was discharging into the river under Westminster Bridge. The malodorous gas from this sewer was so dreadful that it extinguished the lamps of the investigating party. Many of the underground apartments were found to be little more than open cesspools.

Parliament Square 1890 L130008
This monumental clock tower, surmounted by a richly-decorated belfry and spire, is known more popularly as Big Ben, and was designed by E B Denison in 1858 after considerable technical difficulties. The great bell, weighing sixteen tons, was cast at Stockton-on-Tees. It is thought that the clock tower was named after Sir Benjamin Hall, the Commissioner of Works for the project.

◄ **County Hall c1955**
L1305043
This colossal building,
once home of the
controversial Greater
London Council, was
designed by Ralph Knott
and begun in 1912.
Though it sits heavily on
the Embankment, its
broad facades and
massed arches in the
Piranesi style bring it a
monumental dignity.

◀ Lambeth Palace c1955
L1305068

On the south bank of the Thames, opposite the Palace of Westminster is this handsome building, for centuries the official residence of the Archbishops of Canterbury. The entrance is through a Gothic gateway, the ground floor of which was once a prison. The Lollard's Tower adjoins the west end of the chapel. Here the Lollards, followers of Wycliffe, were imprisoned and tortured.

▼ Parliament Street 1908
L130039

Here Parliament Street runs into the spacious thoroughfare of Whitehall which rushes onwards to join Trafalgar Square. On the extreme left is the diminutive gabled roof of the Horse Guards. Whitehall is the traditional home of the offices of government and here are the Treasury, the Home Office, the Privy Council and, of course, the entrance to Downing Street.

◀ Parliament Street and Whitehall 1880 L130016

Serious building work is in progress in this normally sedate street. On the extreme right an area has been cordoned off with barriers, and beyond are the towers of hoists and cranes. Steam funnels into the sky from stationery engines and, in the foreground, a handcart is piled high with bricks. The rush-hour traffic presses a way through as best it can.

Covent Garden Market 1900 L130025
The cries of traders echo through the expansive square, planned by Inigo Jones. The scene has been described by a contemporary guidebook: 'All night long the rumble of heavy wagons seldom ceases, and before daylight the market is crowded. The very loading of these wagons is a wonder, and the wall-like regularity with which cabbages, cauliflowers and turnips are built up to a height of some twelve feet is nothing short of a miracle'.

Flower Sellers, Covent Garden 1885 L130216
The flower market was no less frenetic. 'In spring time it is occupied by dealers in spring and bedding flowers, and the pavement is aglow with colour of flower and leaf, and in the early summer hundreds of women and girls are busily occupied in shelling peas'.

Flower Sellers, Covent Garden 1877 L130117
Flower girls were often orphans, boarding in rooms crowded with other street-sellers. Mayhew reports that they sold violets, wall-flowers, stocks, pinks and roses - anything, in fact, that could be forced and was sweet-smelling. 'Gentlemen are our best customers. Ladies have sometimes said: "A penny, my poor girls, here's three-halfpence for the bunch". Or they have given me the price of two bunches for one.'

Charing Cross 1890

L130180

The cross that gave the area its name was destroyed in 1647. From this point all distances in London are measured. Moreover, a line drawn through it is said to separate the London of pleasure and fashion from that of work and business. The railway station occupies the ground floor of the prestigious company-owned Charing Cross Hotel.

◀ **The Strand 1890** L130005
The Strand stretches from
Temple Bar in the east to
Trafalgar Square in the west.
The beautiful church of
St Clement Danes bestrides
its centre, and was erected
in 1688 from a design by
Wren. The mighty tower was
added by Gibbs in 1719.
It was said that there was
'somehow a greater
lightness and gaiety' here
than you would find a few
hundred yards further
where the city workers
toiled 'with their hurried
walk and preoccupied look'.

◄ The Strand 1890 L130033

From early morning until midnight, The Strand is London's busiest street and invariably congested with traffic. It was originally the waterside thoroughfare between the City and Westminster, and it is from this that it derives its name. In earlier days The Strand was a threatening neighbourhood, and many travellers preferred to take a boat rather than pick their way along the ill-paved street and be jostled by pickpockets.

▼ The Strand 1915 L130191

The Gaiety Theatre dominates the corner where the Aldwych breaks off from the Strand. Theatre goers were enjoying performances by Jose Collins in 'Our Nell'. The glittering building was designed by the very fashionable architect Norman Shaw and opened to theatre goers in 1903. It replaced an older theatre of the same name set between Wellington Street and Catherine Street.

◄ The Aldwych c1920
L130304

Five years on from the previous photograph, the play showing at the Gaiety Theatre is 'Love Lies' starring Stanley Lupino. The Aldwych sweeps off sharply to the north towards Kingsway, leaving an island of fine buildings between it and the Strand. The scheme for the development of the locality was completed in 1905, involving the demolition of twenty-eight acres of crooked lanes and ways.

The City

In 1800 the City coughed under a pall of smoke. It was described as 'a hotch potch of half-moon and serpentine narrow streets, close, dismal, long lanes, stinking allies, dark, gloomy courts and suffocating yards'. Here were the homes and businesses of small shopmen and of the countless craftsmen who laboured in their dark, close workshops.

Once the square mile of the City had been the heart and soul of London. Since the Great Fire city merchants had lived graceful lives in grand houses here. They had powered the creation of Britain's Empire. In the 19th century all this was to change as the money industries swelled and the City became financier to the world. Burgeoning institutions and companies demanded and were granted ever greater space. Whole neighbourhoods of the old City were demolished to make way for sham-Gothic office buildings. In 1850 there had been 130,000 residents. By 1900 the figure had sunk to 27,000. The square mile throbbed with industry during the day but was silent and empty at night.

Temple Bar 1875 L130141
This imposing, ornate gateway once stood where the Strand becomes Fleet Street, and was erected in 1672 to a design by Wren. The effigies portray Stuart monarchs. Beneath its arch Queen Victoria and Albert passed on their way to State services at St Paul's. By the 1860s it was causing considerable traffic congestion and there were heated debates in the press about its future. It was finally removed in 1878 and re-erected at Waltham Cross.

▼ **The Old Curiosity Shop c1955** L1305039

This quaint old house sits on a corner in Lincoln's Inn Fields. It has been claimed, probably erroneously, that it is the original of 'the Old Curiosity Shop' made immortal by Dickens as the home of 'Little Nell'. In this 1950s view it has become an exclusive antique shop but in Victorian times it was a rather dingy emporium owned by H Poole, a jobbing stationer.

▼ **Holborn 1890** L130069

This renowned thoroughfare, a continuation of Oxford Street, links the West End with the City. It takes its name from the Oldbourne Bridge which once spanned the Fleet River. At the foot of the picture is a brewer's dray with stretched canvas tilt. Bowler-hatted clerks enjoy some refreshing breezes on the upper deck of horse-drawn buses.

▲ **Staple Inn c1875**
L130136
Opposite Gray's Inn Road is Staple Inn. It was once the meeting place for wool merchants with a custom house where wool dues were collected. Originally the exclusive province of lawyers, in later years many celebrated figures took rooms in the building, including Dr Johnson, who wrote 'Rasselas' here to help defray his mother's funeral expenses.

◄ Staple Inn c1886 L130174
The magnificent frontage of half-timbered work is the finest in London. Here the plaster rendering shown in the previous photograph has been stripped off revealing a wealth of timbers. The shops have been considerably smartened up. New buildings flank it on both sides, that on the right housing a discount bookshop.

Fleet Street 1890 L130080

'The newest fashion newspaper and the oldest-style tavern still jostle each other now as they did a century or more ago.' This bustling street was once the home of the British press. The working day here ran for a full twenty-four hours, with printers and reporters crowding the bars day and night. Crowning the scene in the distance is the glorious dome of St Paul's.

King's Cross Station c1886 L130067

This London terminus of the Great Northern Railway was opened in 1852. It was built on the site of the old Smallpox Hospital. Its twin brick arches, surmounted by a central clock tower, make it a curiously modern-looking building. There was a granary here that would accept 60,000 sacks of corn, water-tanks holding 150,000 gallons and a goods shed 600 feet long. From King's Cross trains plied the east coast route to Scotland.

St John's Gate, Clerkenwell c1886 L130144
The old gateway to the priory of the Knights of St John stands in St John's Lane, south of the Clerkenwell Road. In the late Gothic style and built with rough-faced stone from a Kent quarry, it was erected by Prior Docwra in 1504. The Old Jerusalem Tavern occupies the ground floor.

Peter's Lane, Clerkenwell Road 1880 L130096
Close by St John's Gate is this narrow alley of tall tile-hung shops and houses, which lean precariously over so that residents might almost stretch out and shake hands from their windows. Clerkenwell was the neighbourhood where the jewellers, watchmakers and silversmiths of the City had their workshops. It is said there was always the stench of seal oil, used to lubricate clocks and watches.

Ludgate Hill 1897 L130037
A locomotive of the L. C. & D Railway has just left Holborn Viaduct Station and thunders south over the bridge, steam ballooning out over the roofs. Below, traffic crawls miserably up Ludgate Hill. In wet weather horses with heavy wagons slipped and slid up to St Paul's. The quagmire became so impassable that a new wooden roadway had to be added.

▼ **New Bridge Street and Queen Victoria Street 1904** L130306
The Hand-in-Hand Fire and Life Insurance Society building stands at the
junction of these two streets close by Blackfriars Bridge. It was established
in 1696 and by 1890 had amassed accumulated funds of over two million
pounds. To its right is the railway bridge from Holborn Viaduct Station.

▼ **Oxford Arms, Warwick Lane c1875** L130122
This old inn has been serving clients since 1673, and was once an important
coaching stop. In the 1860s, after the demise of the stages, many of its rooms
were let out to lodgers. However, it was still a strategic terminus for carriers
plying between London, Oxford and other regional towns. It finally shut its
doors in 1875 and was demolished.

▲ **St Paul's from Across
the River 1890** L130126
This panoramic vista of
the City and St Paul's was
probably taken from the
southern tip of Southwark
Bridge. In early days
Queenhithe on the north
bank of the Thames was a
significant port for the
landing of fish and corn.
Its position above London
Bridge - the successful
docks were all in broader
reaches down-river - led
to its inevitable decline.

◀ **St Paul's Cathedral 1890**

L130078

Perched on the summit of Ludgate Hill at almost the highest point in the City, Wren's masterpiece is the pride of London. In the form of a cross, it is built in the Corinthian style, and surmounted by the giant dome which rises on arches over the centre. Many great men and women are buried here, including Wren himself, James Barry, Sir Joshua Reynolds, Opie and Landseer.

Queen Victoria Street 1897 L130055
The heart of the Square Mile. City life looks as frenetic as it does today. Job mobility was unheard of in the Victorian office. Only by staying with the same employer was there any hope of security and a modest pension. The best positions were with banks and insurance offices. Those keen to climb the career ladder avoided Law Chambers, which paid the meanest salaries.

St Paul's from Cannon Street 1905 L130164
The magnificent elevations of St Paul's soar above the surrounding streets. Wren directed its construction at such a ponderous pace that Parliament cut his salary from £200 to £100 a year. It was not until 1711, when the work was finally completed, that he was repaid the balance owing. In the street the modest cart of the 'People's Caterers' is offering 'machine-made bread'. At the time mechanisation was the way to the future and constituted a distinct trading advantage.

Cheapside c1886 L130066

In the 1850s, Cheapside was one of the most fashionable shopping streets in London, with a 'mighty stream of traffic' flowing through from Oxford Street to Leadenhall and the City. Because of its prestigious reputation and close proximity to the Bank, city financiers clamoured to live here, and annual rents from a single house could reach the incredible sum of three hundred pounds.

Cheapside c1905 L130273

At the junction with Paternoster Row, Cheapside swings from the north in an arc and heads east towards the Bank. Paternoster Row, on the right, was once a fashionable shopping street patronised by Pepys and his wife. Nicholson, the haberdasher and milliner on the corner, has an impressive new frontage constructed in 1900.

◀ **Mansion House and Cheapside c1890** L130177
In the distance, the graceful Portland stone spire of St Mary le Bow soars sublimely over the City. It was the most expensive of Wren's refurbishments, costing £15,400. The ponderous Victorian Gothic architecture of this part of the City is not to everyone's taste today. Mappin and Webb's corner premises, together with the section of Queen Victoria Street down to Cannon Street, were completed in 1869.

Mansion House and Cheapside 1890 L130209
Mansion House, the lavish building on the left, has been the official residence of the Lord Mayor for two centuries. It was built by George Dance on the site of the old stocks market. It has been said to have the air of a Roman palazzo. The portico is reached by flights of stone steps from the pavement and, from under the fluted columns, city workers could watch the throng of traffic passing below.

Mansion House and Cheapside 1915 L130192
The foundation stone of the Mansion House was laid in 1739. The facade is so hemmed in by the street and the buildings opposite that it could never achieve the visual impact its architects would have wished for. The buses chugging along below are still open-topped. It would be another ten years before roofs were added to the London General Omnibus Company's fleets.

The Bank of England and the Royal Exchange 1890 L130208
Richard Jefferies described the scene in the 1880s: 'Like the spokes of a wheel converging, streams of human life flow into this agitated pool... Blue carts and yellow omnibuses, varnished carriages and brown vans, pale loads of yellow straw ... this is the vortex and whirlpool, the centre of human life today on the earth'.

The Bank of England 1890 L130179
Opposite the Mansion House is the Bank of England, a single-storey monolithic edifice, designed in 1734 by George Sampson. Sir John Soane devised some alterations to the west elevation in 1788. In late Victorian times there were nine hundred employees with salaries ranging from £50 to £1,200. The total salary bill was £210,000 - the sum a single top manager might earn today!

▼ **The Bank of England and the Royal Exchange 1908** L130153
In the late 19th century a commentator pointed out that 'the stranger will be particularly struck with the absence of women from the moving crowd in Cheapside, and indeed generally in the City'. This was to change very soon: young women would soon be taking over the office desks as typing-pools were established - the first typewriter appeared in the 1880s.

▼ **The Bank of England and the Royal Exchange c1910** L130207
In the 1860s the economist Bagehot described Lombard Street, that runs to the right of the Mansion House, as 'by far the greatest combination of economical power and economic delicacy that the world has ever seen'. With the coming of the railways and international currency dealings, the City began to prosper as it never had before, with small investors flocking to involve themselves in the heady world of stocks and shares.

▲ **The Bank of England and the Royal Exchange 1886** L130181
In 1838 there was a great conflagration which began in the rooms of Lloyd's coffee-house. Thousands of tons of masonry fell and the old Royal Exchange was destroyed. The new Exchange was designed by William Tite and built at a furious pace. Within three years it was open for business. Chantrey's equestrian statue of the Duke of Wellington erected in the broad space created.

◄ Threadneedle Street and the Royal Exchange c1910 L130193
Omnibuses advertising Dunlop tyres enter Threadneedle Street. Here was the famous American Coffee House, where merchants with interests in the colonies met to discuss business. On the right is horse-drawn cart of the Royal Mail.

The Royal Exchange 1886 L130012
The frieze that tops the Corinthian portico proclaims in Latin that the Exchange was founded in the thirteenth year of Queen Elizabeth, and restored in the seventh of Queen Victoria. The pediment above features figures sculpted by Richard Westmacott, representing Commerce holding the charter of the Exchange, attended by the Lord Mayor and merchants.

The Monument c1890 L130187
At the foot of King William Street is Wren's mighty fluted Doric column of Portland stone, erected to commemorate the Great Fire of London in 1666. It was one of the tourist attractions of the City to climb to the top, and in 1842 rails were added to the lofty gallery to prevent suicides. In 'Martin Chuzzlewit' the keeper considered it 'quite worth twice the money not to make the ascent'.

King William Street 1880 L130102

This photograph shows the Cannon Street end of King William Street, which heads south-east from the Mansion House towards London Bridge. This dignified thoroughfare was conceived in 1835, and was much admired for its spacious and airy atmosphere. On the left is the City Luncheon Bar, and in the foreground a fleet of carrier's carts owned by Henry Drapper.

London Bridge 1890 L130018

In the background is the Monument, rising over the roofs of Adelaide House, home of the Pearl Assurance Company. This squat building was demolished in 1920, and underneath was found one of the arches of the old London Bridge. London Bridge would seem to have been closed off to traffic.

The King's Head, Borough High Street 1875 L130131
This old inn, just over the river from London Bridge, was called by Stow 'one of the fair inns' of Southwark. In 1720 it was described as 'well built, handsome, and enjoying a good trade'. In this view it looks a ramshackle establishment, with Chinese-style latticed balconies and shabby cellars. It had shut up shop by 1885.

The Tower Of London c1920 L130251
This stunning panorama looks south-east over the battlements and roofs of London's most celebrated building and towards the river and Tower Bridge. The pinnacles of the White Tower pierce the city sky.

◄ **The Tower of London c1890** L130172
This ancient fortress has served as arsenal, prison and royal residence, and is comprised of an irregular mass of buildings erected at various periods down the centuries. It was begun by William Conqueror, and it is his keep, the White Tower, that still dominates the scene. The moat was drained in 1843 and sown with grasses and shrubs.

◀ The Tower of London c1955

L1305022

Tugs towing flat-bottomed barges are still plying the Thames in this 1950s scene. Seventy years before there was a timber quay under the walls of the Tower, with tall-masted sailing ships edging through the raised bascules of Tower Bridge. The river here was thick with islands of logs chained together, floating heavily in the shallows.

▼ The Tower Of London c1920 L130251

This stunning panorama looks south-east over the battlements and roofs of London's most celebrated building and towards the river and Tower Bridge. The pinnacles of the White Tower pierce the city sky.

◀ The Elephant and Castle c1890 L130028

This crowded region south of the river was once the heart of London cockney life. The Elephant and Castle, a great meeting place of thoroughfares, was termed a 'ganglion of roads' by Dickens in 'Bleak House'. The squat old inn that gave it its name dominates the scene, and is offering hot and cold joints, chops and steaks to diners.

The Crystal Palace

This monumental glass pleasure dome was created in Hyde Park by Joseph Paxton for the Great Exhibition of 1851. 2,000 workers erected it at high speed, bolting and welding together 3,300 iron columns, 205 miles of sash-bars and 293,655 panes of glass! It was a temple to the triumphs of Victorian art and industry. After the Exhibition, it was moved to wooded parkland at Sydenham in south-east London.

Crystal Palace 1900 L130147

Crystal Palace c1890 L130059
Pleasure seekers make the most of the winter weather skating on one of the many lakes. The Crystal Palace became a paradise for Londoners keen to escape the dirt and the grime. At weekends they flocked to Sydenham in their thousands to enjoy the displays and exhibitions - Blondin once walked a high wire here and cooked an omelette seventy feet in the air!

Crystal Palace 1890 L130060
This ornate pleasure craft looks perilously low in the water, but the throng of passengers seem quite oblivious of the rising water levels. Queen Victoria was a regular visitor to the Crystal Palace, and once encouraged the Shah of Persia to sample its delights. These pleasure grounds were an unparalleled symbol of the continuing glories and achievements of her reign.

A Tavern Scene 1885 L130210
The public house has long been a vital constituent of city life. Here customers could relax after the day's toil with a tankard of porter. In the Victorian era the tavern became the exclusive haunt of the poor. The coming of the notorious gin-houses, combined with Victorian prudery and fears of vice, encouraged the more well-to-do to frequent safer restaurants and hotels. As Dickens pointed out: 'Gin drinking is a great vice in England'. The simple pleasure of a pot and a pipe were largely ousted.

Diamond Jubilee

Queen Victoria lived from 1819 to 1901. Her reign spanned two generations. By 1850 her loyal subjects had borrowed their sovereign's name and were calling themselves 'Victorians'. The young and popular Queen reigned over a land that ruled the world, and her subjects were proud of her and of their country's achievements and potential. Britain was in the midst of creating the world's first great industrial power and it necessarily involved a process of upheaval and social change.

Inherent was a deep-ingrained instinct for nationalism which bonded the nation together in difficult and troublesome times. The Victorians were never slow in celebrating a civic occasion, and thronged the streets whenever a gesture of loyalty to queen and country was required. It is not surprising, therefore, that when the time of her Diamond Jubilee came around that the whole of London flocked to honour her. They cheered the military and its colourful pageantry, the endless procession of carriages containing dignitaries. 'Vanity Fair' pronounced on the day's proceedings: 'We are a great people and we realised it on Saturday as we never realised it before'.

The Albert Memorial 1897 L130011
Crowds gather on the steps of Gilbert Scott's imposing Gothic-inspired memorial to the Queen's beloved husband, Albert. The Guards' bandsmen, resplendent in busbies and bright red uniforms, are waiting to begin their procession.

◀ **Buckingham Palace 1897** L130157
The royal coach heads out across the courtyard of the Palace bound for The Mall. A throng of carriages waits to join the procession across London. Queen Victoria wrote in her diary that it was 'a never-to-be-forgotten day... No one ever, I believe, has met with such an ovation as was given to me ... Every face seemed to be filled with real joy'.

◄ Westminster Bridge 1897 L130219
Jubilee day was the perfect occasion for royal pageantry. After a service at St Paul's, the ageing Queen was driven in her state coach past Parliament and across this crowded bridge, escorted by her loyal troops. The bridge is decked with garlands.

▼ Diamond Jubilee Day 1897 L130158
Queen Victoria smiles graciously at her subjects from beneath a parasol. The team of horses bend under the weight of shining brasses and decorative tackle. Behind the coach stand a gathering of be-robed dignitaries of the Church.

◄ City Scene 1897 L130010
One of the great city institutions, possibly the Mansion House, is hung with swags of flowers and garlands for the great occasion. The porch has a decorative pelmet embroidered with a message celebrating the sixty glorious years of her reign. A crowd has gathered outside, anxious to catch a glimpse of their sovereign and to catch a few words of the ceremony.

Street Characters

The streets of London were thick with beggars and confidence tricksters. A guidebook in 1888 suggested the following action be taken by travellers if they were accosted: 'To get rid of your beggar, when wearisome, take no notice of him at all. He will follow you till you meet a more likely person, but no farther'. Yet many beggars were making desperate efforts to lift themselves and their families out of unrelenting poverty by taking on a trade, however small. The match sellers, shoe blacks and flower girls, many displaced from the countryside where life was yet more unendurable, were given short shrift by many of the great and wealthy. The same guide suggests: 'If your tormentor has anything to sell, reply simply, "Got one," and pass on'.

Street traders faced suspicion from the public and persecution by the police on a daily basis. Their lives were a continual struggle to win food and shelter. Many lived in cheap, overcrowded lodging houses in poor areas of the West End and the City, where they were preyed upon by voracious landlords. There was, of course, no social relief, and families were forced back on their own cunning and guile to keep body and soul together.

The Organ Grinder 1895 L130109
The barrel organ always drew a huge crowd with its wheezy renderings of popular tunes. When a trio of frightened monkeys was introduced the attraction for children was irresistible. Here they crowd closely round while the monkeys, dressed in waistcoats are goaded reluctantly into performing their tricks.

The Match Seller 1884 L130116
Selling a few lucifers was all too often the pretext for begging. Bryant and May employed seven hundred girls to sell their matches on the streets. In 1888 these girls went on strike for better pay and conditions. Such a protest and threat to public order was rare amongst itinerant workers.

The Boardman 1877 L130118
Employing the services of a boardman was a popular means of advertising for the Victorian shopman. For a few pence this old man walked the fashionable shopping streets of the West End proffering his handbills. On the wooden palm attached to his hat Renovo have printed their sales slogan.

Ginger Cake Seller 1884 L130111
This dark-coloured cake of flour, treacle and ground ginger was a favourite snack with Victorians at fairs and street events. The roughly-shaped pieces were measured into paper cones. This old man's gingercake was probably made by his wife or daughters.

The Water Seller c1890 L1302002
There were continual public fears about the purity of London's water supply. In early Victorian times water taken from the Thames at Chelsea was infected with the contents of the city's sewers and the drainings from its dunghills. There were terrible widespread cholera outbreaks in the 1840s and 50s. The water seller shown here would have had a regular pitch so that clients grew to trust the purity of his water.

Shoeblacks c1890 L130119
By the 1880s the shoeblack societies had four hundred boys on their books. A number were given cheap board and lodging. These shoeblacks were licensed to trade by the Metropolitan Police and carried on their business unhindered. There were, however, many unofficial operators, who 'infested the streets and annoyed the passenger'.

The Bootblack 1895 L130114
The bootblack business grew into a highly-organised and philanthropic affair. Sporting their red uniforms, the bootblack boys were a familiar sight on the streets of London. The Ragged Schools, Saffron Hill, set up the first society, and nine others followed. The aim was to educate orphan boys and to give them a good start in the world.

The Dancing Bear 1895 L130108
Bears had long been abused by Londoners. In the 17th century there was a popular bear garden at Bankside. This poor creature is urged to dance to bugle tunes played by his owner, who is probably an old soldier. Though tightly muzzled, this giant seven-foot bear must have terrified passers-by, as he complained at his miserable lot.

The Newspaper Seller c1890 L1302004
A bewildering number of morning and evening newspapers was available to the Victorian reading public, including the Daily Chronicle, the Times, the Evening News and the Morning Advertiser. In the 1880s and 90s, new printing technology released onto the market a wide range of cheap and tacky weekly magazines and comics. This old newspaper woman stands her ground under the spinning wheels of passing carriages.

**The Potato Seller
c1890** L1302001
This street trading
woman is offering
potatoes from her
basket. Baked potatoes
were even more popular
with Londoners, and
handcarts fitted with
ovens and chimneys
plied the streets offering
inexpensive hot snacks.
She looks relaxed
enough but the weight of
the potatoes must be
excruciating.

▼ **Hokey Pokey Stall , Greenwich 1884** L130110
Children cluster round licking at the cheap ice cream from the hokey
pokey stall. They look like ragged street urchins in their rumpled suits
and battered boots, and were probably bought their treats in return
for posing for the photographer.

▼ **The Chair Mender 1877** L130112
There were once 2,500 cabinet-making shops in London, many employing
children. When steam-powered sawmills and mechanical production
methods introduced ready-made furniture onto the market, thousands of
craftsmen lost their jobs. Here, an old man re-canes a child's chair.

▲ **The Strawberry Seller
1885** L130213
This rather forlorn picture
shows a tiny emaciated
pony pulling a cart selling
strawberries. We associate
this exotic and scarce fruit
with jollity and celebration,
but this trader and her son
radiate only a sense of
misery and poverty.

◀ **The Cutler 1890** L130167
The late Victorian era was one of immense change. Machines had taken over the production of many household gadgets that had been previously made by individual craftsmen. This mechanisation caused terrible unemployment. Many older tradesmen, unable to find work, took to the streets with their handcarts.

The Chimney Sweep 1884 L130115
Mayhew reports that sweepers were a tight-knit community. Master sweepers often let room to families in the same trade. The climbing boys, often from the Workhouse, earned 2d or 3d a day, but were sometimes given an extra 6d by grateful householders. They climbed easily up through wide flues using their elbows and legs, but often got stuck or nearly suffocated in narrow nine-inch chimneys.

The Knife Sharpener, Whitechapel Road 1885 L130214
This cutler and locksmith has an established stall in the market in the Whitechapel Road. He is a general jobber, able to sharpen knives and tools, re-set saws, repair locks and cut replacement keys. Hanging on the rail behind are huge clumps of keys.

Nomads 1885 L130212

Vagrants have wandered the fields and lanes of Britain down the centuries. Subject to no laws they were the truly free people of the world. The Vagrancy Act of 1824 made it illegal for them to be out in the open air without visible means of subsistence. Life became suddenly more complicated. The Reading-style caravan in the photograph was a new introduction. Families followed the country fairs and markets and often ventured into London for the festivals and fairs held on the commons.

Index

Frith Book Co Titles

www.francisfrith.co.uk

The Frith Book Company publishes over 100 new titles each year. A selection of those currently available are listed below. For latest catalogue please contact Frith Book Co.

Town Books 96 pages, approx 100 photos. County and Themed Books 128 pages, approx 150 photos (unless specified). All titles hardback laminated case and jacket except those indicated pb (paperback)

Amersham, Chesham & Rickmansworth (pb)		
	1-85937-340-2	£9.99
Ancient Monuments & Stone Circles	1-85937-143-4	£17.99
Aylesbury (pb)	1-85937-227-9	£9.99
Bakewell	1-85937-113-2	£12.99
Barnstaple (pb)	1-85937-300-3	£9.99
Bath (pb)	1-85937-419-0	£9.99
Bedford (pb)	1-85937-205-8	£9.99
Berkshire (pb)	1-85937-191-4	£9.99
Berkshire Churches	1-85937-170-1	£17.99
Blackpool (pb)	1-85937-382-8	£9.99
Bognor Regis (pb)	1-85937-431-x	£9.99
Bournemouth	1-85937-067-5	£12.99
Bradford (pb)	1-85937-204-x	£9.99
Brighton & Hove(pb)	1-85937-192-2	£8.99
Bristol (pb)	1-85937-264-3	£9.99
British Life A Century Ago (pb)	1-85937-213-9	£9.99
Buckinghamshire (pb)	1-85937-200-7	£9.99
Camberley (pb)	1-85937-222-8	£9.99
Cambridge (pb)	1-85937-422-0	£9.99
Cambridgeshire (pb)	1-85937-420-4	£9.99
Canals & Waterways (pb)	1-85937-291-0	£9.99
Canterbury Cathedral (pb)	1-85937-179-5	£9.99
Cardiff (pb)	1-85937-093-4	£9.99
Carmarthenshire	1-85937-216-3	£14.99
Chelmsford (pb)	1-85937-310-0	£9.99
Cheltenham (pb)	1-85937-095-0	£9.99
Cheshire (pb)	1-85937-271-6	£9.99
Chester	1-85937-090-x	£12.99
Chesterfield	1-85937-378-x	£9.99
Chichester (pb)	1-85937-228-7	£9.99
Colchester (pb)	1-85937-188-4	£8.99
Cornish Coast	1-85937-163-9	£14.99
Cornwall (pb)	1-85937-229-5	£9.99
Cornwall Living Memories	1-85937-248-1	£14.99
Cotswolds (pb)	1-85937-230-9	£9.99
Cotswolds Living Memories	1-85937-255-4	£14.99
County Durham	1-85937-123-x	£14.99
Croydon Living Memories	1-85937-162-0	£9.99
Cumbria	1-85937-101-9	£14.99
Dartmoor	1-85937-145-0	£14.99
Derby (pb)	1-85937-367-4	£9.99
Derbyshire (pb)	1-85937-196-5	£9.99
Devon (pb)	1-85937-297-x	£9.99
Dorset (pb)	1-85937-269-4	£9.99
Dorset Churches	1-85937-172-8	£17.99
Dorset Coast (pb)	1-85937-299-6	£9.99
Dorset Living Memories	1-85937-210-4	£14.99
Down the Severn	1-85937-118-3	£14.99
Down the Thames (pb)	1-85937-278-3	£9.99
Down the Trent	1-85937-311-9	£14.99
Dublin (pb)	1-85937-231-7	£9.99
East Anglia (pb)	1-85937-265-1	£9.99
East London	1-85937-080-2	£14.99
East Sussex	1-85937-130-2	£14.99
Eastbourne	1-85937-061-6	£12.99
Edinburgh (pb)	1-85937-193-0	£8.99
England in the 1880s	1-85937-331-3	£17.99
English Castles (pb)	1-85937-434-4	£9.99
English Country Houses	1-85937-161-2	£17.99
Essex (pb)	1-85937-270-8	£9.99
Exeter	1-85937-126-4	£12.99
Exmoor	1-85937-132-9	£14.99
Falmouth	1-85937-066-7	£12.99
Folkestone (pb)	1-85937-124-8	£9.99
Glasgow (pb)	1-85937-190-6	£9.99
Gloucestershire	1-85937-102-7	£14.99
Great Yarmouth (pb)	1-85937-426-3	£9.99
Greater Manchester (pb)	1-85937-266-x	£9.99
Guildford (pb)	1-85937-410-7	£9.99
Hampshire (pb)	1-85937-279-1	£9.99
Hampshire Churches (pb)	1-85937-207-4	£9.99
Harrogate	1-85937-423-9	£9.99
Hastings & Bexhill (pb)	1-85937-131-0	£9.99
Heart of Lancashire (pb)	1-85937-197-3	£9.99
Helston (pb)	1-85937-214-7	£9.99
Hereford (pb)	1-85937-175-2	£9.99
Herefordshire	1-85937-174-4	£14.99
Hertfordshire (pb)	1-85937-247-3	£9.99
Horsham (pb)	1-85937-432-8	£9.99
Humberside	1-85937-215-5	£14.99
Hythe, Romney Marsh & Ashford	1-85937-256-2	£9.99

Available from your local bookshop or from the publisher

Frith Book Co Titles (continued)

Ipswich (pb)	1-85937-424-7	£9.99	St Ives (pb)	1-85937415-8	£9.99
Ireland (pb)	1-85937-181-7	£9.99	Scotland (pb)	1-85937-182-5	£9.99
Isle of Man (pb)	1-85937-268-6	£9.99	Scottish Castles (pb)	1-85937-323-2	£9.99
Isles of Scilly	1-85937-136-1	£14.99	Sevenoaks & Tunbridge	1-85937-057-8	£12.99
Isle of Wight (pb)	1-85937-429-8	£9.99	Sheffield, South Yorks (pb)	1-85937-267-8	£9.99
Isle of Wight Living Memories	1-85937-304-6	£14.99	Shrewsbury (pb)	1-85937-325-9	£9.99
Kent (pb)	1-85937-189-2	£9.99	Shropshire (pb)	1-85937-326-7	£9.99
Kent Living Memories	1-85937-125-6	£14.99	Somerset	1-85937-153-1	£14.99
Lake District (pb)	1-85937-275-9	£9.99	South Devon Coast	1-85937-107-8	£14.99
Lancaster, Morecambe & Heysham (pb)	1-85937-233-3	£9.99	South Devon Living Memories	1-85937-168-x	£14.99
Leeds (pb)	1-85937-202-3	£9.99	South Hams	1-85937-220-1	£14.99
Leicester	1-85937-073-x	£12.99	Southampton (pb)	1-85937-427-1	£9.99
Leicestershire (pb)	1-85937-185-x	£9.99	Southport (pb)	1-85937-425-5	£9.99
Lincolnshire (pb)	1-85937-433-6	£9.99	Staffordshire	1-85937-047-0	£12.99
Liverpool & Merseyside (pb)	1-85937-234-1	£9.99	Stratford upon Avon	1-85937-098-5	£12.99
London (pb)	1-85937-183-3	£9.99	Suffolk (pb)	1-85937-221-x	£9.99
Ludlow (pb)	1-85937-176-0	£9.99	Suffolk Coast	1-85937-259-7	£14.99
Luton (pb)	1-85937-235-x	£9.99	Surrey (pb)	1-85937-240-6	£9.99
Maidstone	1-85937-056-x	£14.99	Sussex (pb)	1-85937-184-1	£9.99
Manchester (pb)	1-85937-198-1	£9.99	Swansea (pb)	1-85937-167-1	£9.99
Middlesex	1-85937-158-2	£14.99	Tees Valley & Cleveland	1-85937-211-2	£14.99
New Forest	1-85937-128-0	£14.99	Thanet (pb)	1-85937-116-7	£9.99
Newark (pb)	1-85937-366-6	£9.99	Tiverton (pb)	1-85937-178-7	£9.99
Newport, Wales (pb)	1-85937-258-9	£9.99	Torbay	1-85937-063-2	£12.99
Newquay (pb)	1-85937-421-2	£9.99	Truro	1-85937-147-7	£12.99
Norfolk (pb)	1-85937-195-7	£9.99	Victorian and Edwardian Cornwall	1-85937-252-x	£14.99
Norfolk Living Memories	1-85937-217-1	£14.99	Victorian & Edwardian Devon	1-85937-253-8	£14.99
Northamptonshire	1-85937-150-7	£14.99	Victorian & Edwardian Kent	1-85937-149-3	£14.99
Northumberland Tyne & Wear (pb)	1-85937-281-3	£9.99	Vic & Ed Maritime Album	1-85937-144-2	£17.99
North Devon Coast	1-85937-146-9	£14.99	Victorian and Edwardian Sussex	1-85937-157-4	£14.99
North Devon Living Memories	1-85937-261-9	£14.99	Victorian & Edwardian Yorkshire	1-85937-154-x	£14.99
North London	1-85937-206-6	£14.99	Victorian Seaside	1-85937-159-0	£17.99
North Wales (pb)	1-85937-298-8	£9.99	Villages of Devon (pb)	1-85937-293-7	£9.99
North Yorkshire (pb)	1-85937-236-8	£9.99	Villages of Kent (pb)	1-85937-294-5	£9.99
Norwich (pb)	1-85937-194-9	£8.99	Villages of Sussex (pb)	1-85937-295-3	£9.99
Nottingham (pb)	1-85937-324-0	£9.99	Warwickshire (pb)	1-85937-203-1	£9.99
Nottinghamshire (pb)	1-85937-187-6	£9.99	Welsh Castles (pb)	1-85937-322-4	£9.99
Oxford (pb)	1-85937-411-5	£9.99	West Midlands (pb)	1-85937-289-9	£9.99
Oxfordshire (pb)	1-85937-430-1	£9.99	West Sussex	1-85937-148-5	£14.99
Peak District (pb)	1-85937-280-5	£9.99	West Yorkshire (pb)	1-85937-201-5	£9.99
Penzance	1-85937-069-1	£12.99	Weymouth (pb)	1-85937-209-0	£9.99
Peterborough (pb)	1-85937-219-8	£9.99	Wiltshire (pb)	1-85937-277-5	£9.99
Piers	1-85937-237-6	£17.99	Wiltshire Churches (pb)	1-85937-171-x	£9.99
Plymouth	1-85937-119-1	£12.99	Wiltshire Living Memories	1-85937-245-7	£14.99
Poole & Sandbanks (pb)	1-85937-251-1	£9.99	Winchester (pb)	1-85937-428-x	£9.99
Preston (pb)	1-85937-212-0	£9.99	Windmills & Watermills	1-85937-242-2	£17.99
Reading (pb)	1-85937-238-4	£9.99	Worcester (pb)	1-85937-165-5	£9.99
Romford (pb)	1-85937-319-4	£9.99	Worcestershire	1-85937-152-3	£14.99
Salisbury (pb)	1-85937-239-2	£9.99	York (pb)	1-85937-199-x	£9.99
Scarborough (pb)	1-85937-379-8	£9.99	Yorkshire (pb)	1-85937-186-8	£9.99
St Albans (pb)	1-85937-341-0	£9.99	Yorkshire Living Memories	1-85937-166-3	£14.99

See Frith books on the internet www.francisfrith.co.uk

FRITH PRODUCTS & SERVICES

Francis Frith would doubtless be pleased to know that the pioneering publishing venture he started in 1860 still continues today. A hundred and forty years later, The Francis Frith Collection continues in the same innovative tradition and is now one of the foremost publishers of vintage photographs in the world. Some of the current activities include:

Interior Decoration

Today Frith's photographs can be seen framed and as giant wall murals in thousands of pubs, restaurants, hotels, banks, retail stores and other public buildings throughout the country. In every case they enhance the unique local atmosphere of the places they depict and provide reminders of gentler days in an increasingly busy and frenetic world.

Product Promotions

Frith products are used by many major companies to promote the sales of their own products or to reinforce their own history and heritage. Frith promotions have been used by Hovis bread, Courage beers, Scots Porage Oats, Colman's mustard, Cadbury's foods, Mellow Birds coffee, Dunhill pipe tobacco, Guinness, and Bulmer's Cider.

Genealogy and Family History

As the interest in family history and roots grows world-wide, more and more people are turning to Frith's photographs of Great Britain for images of the towns, villages and streets where their ancestors lived; and, of course, photographs of the churches and chapels where their ancestors were christened, married and buried are an essential part of every genealogy tree and family album.

Frith Products

All Frith photographs are available Framed or just as Mounted Prints and Posters (size 23 x 16 inches). These may be ordered from the address below. From time to time other products - Address Books, Calendars, Table Mats, etc - are available.

The Internet

Already twenty thousand Frith photographs can be viewed and purchased on the internet through the Frith websites and a myriad of partner sites.

For more detailed information on Frith companies and products, look at these sites:

www.francisfrith.co.uk
www.francisfrith.com
(for North American visitors)

See the complete list of Frith Books at:

www.francisfrith.co.uk

This web site is regularly updated with the latest list of publications from the Frith Book Company. If you wish to buy books relating to another part of the country that your local bookshop does not stock, you may purchase on-line.

For further information, trade, or author enquiries please contact us at the address below:
The Francis Frith Collection, Frith's Barn, Teffont, Salisbury, Wiltshire, England SP3 5QP.
Tel: +44 (0)1722 716 376 Fax: +44 (0)1722 716 881 Email: sales@francisfrith.co.uk

See Frith books on the internet www.francisfrith.co.uk

TO RECEIVE YOUR FREE MOUNTED PRINT

Mounted Print
Overall size 14 x 11 inches

Cut out this Voucher and return it with your remittance for £1.95 to cover postage and handling, to UK addresses. For overseas addresses please include £4.00 post and handling. Choose any photograph included in this book. Your SEPIA print will be A4 in size, and mounted in a cream mount with burgundy rule line, overall size 14 x 11 inches.

Order additional Mounted Prints at HALF PRICE (only £7.49 each*)

If there are further pictures you would like to order, possibly as gifts for friends and family, purchase them at half price (no additional postage and handling required).

Have your Mounted Prints framed*

For an additional £14.95 per print you can have your chosen Mounted Print framed in an elegant polished wood and gilt moulding, overall size 16 x 13 inches (no additional postage and handling required).

---

* IMPORTANT!
These special prices are only available if ordered using the original voucher on this page (no copies permitted) and at the same time as your free Mounted Print, for delivery to the same address

---

Frith Collectors' Guild

From time to time we publish a magazine of news and stories about Frith photographs and further special offers of Frith products. If you would like 12 months FREE membership, please return this form.

Send completed forms to:
The Francis Frith Collection, Frith's Barn, Teffont, Salisbury, Wiltshire SP3 5QP

Voucher for FREE and Reduced Price Frith Prints

Picture no.	Page number	Qty	Mounted @ £7.49	Framed + £14.95	Total Cost
		1	**Free of charge***	£	£
			£7.49	£	£
			£7.49	£	£
			£7.49	£	£
			£7.49	£	£
			£7.49	£	£

Please allow 28 days for delivery	*** Post & handling**	**£1.95**
Book Title	**Total Order Cost**	**£**

Please do not photocopy this voucher. Only the original is valid, so please cut it out and return it to us.

I enclose a cheque / postal order for £. . . . .
made payable to 'The Francis Frith Collection'
OR please debit my Mastercard / Visa / Switch / Amex card
(credit cards please on all overseas orders)

Number . . . .

Issue No (Switch only) . . . . .Valid from (Amex/Switch) . . . .

Expires . . . . Signature . . . .

Name Mr/Mrs/Ms . . . .

Address . . . .

. . . .

. . . .

. . . . Postcode . . . .

Daytime Tel No . . . . Valid to 31/12/02

The Francis Frith Collectors' Guild

Please enrol me as a member for 12 months free of charge.

Name Mr/Mrs/Ms . . . .

Address . . . .

. . . .

. . . .

. . . . Postcode . . . .

Would you like to find out more about Francis Frith?

We have recently recruited some entertaining speakers who are happy to visit local groups, clubs and societies to give an illustrated talk documenting Frith's travels and photographs. If you are a member of such a group and are interested in hosting a presentation, we would love to hear from you.

Our speakers bring with them a small selection of our local town and county books, together with sample prints. They are happy to take orders. A small proportion of the order value is donated to the group who have hosted the presentation. The talks are therefore an excellent way of fundraising for small groups and societies.

Can you help us with information about any of the Frith photographs in this book?

We are gradually compiling an historical record for each of the photographs in the Frith archive. It is always fascinating to find out the names of the people shown in the pictures, as well as insights into the shops, buildings and other features depicted.

If you recognize anyone in the photographs in this book, or if you have information not already included in the author's caption, do let us know. We would love to hear from you, and will try to publish it in future books or articles.

Our production team

Frith books are produced by a small dedicated team at offices in the converted Grade II listed 18th-century barn at Teffont near Salisbury, illustrated above. Most have worked with the Frith Collection for many years. All have in common one quality: they have a passion for the Frith Collection. The team is constantly expanding, but currently includes:

Jason Buck, John Buck, Douglas Burns, Heather Crisp, Isobel Hall, Rob Hames, Hazel Heaton, Peter Horne, James Kinnear, Tina Leary, Hannah Marsh, Eliza Sackett, Terence Sackett, Sandra Sanger, Shelley Tolcher, Susanna Walker, Clive Wathen and Jenny Wathen.